Commercial Real Estate Financing Fraud

Suspicious Activity Reports by Depository Institutions
January 1, 2007 – December 31, 2010

March 2011

Commercial Real Estate Financing Fraud

Suspicious Activity Reports by Depository Institutions
January 1, 2007 – December 31, 2010

March 2011

Table of Contents

Executive Summary*

The number of depository institution Suspicious Activity Report (SAR) filings reporting commercial real estate financing fraud (hereinafter "CRE fraud") almost tripled between 2007 and 2010, reflecting the challenges facing the commercial real estate (hereinafter "CRE") sector and the ever-present opportunity for fraud. In contrast to mortgage loan fraud SARs predominantly submitted by large financial institutions, filings reporting potential CRE fraud came from institutions of varying sizes and locations, indicating that CRE fraud may affect a broad range of reporting institutions.

CRE loans totaling an estimated $1.4 trillion will reach the end of their terms between 2010 and 2014,[1] and some analysts anticipate a delinquency rate of 10 percent on these loans.[2] Given the size and potential future volatility of the CRE market, SARs may play an important role in providing law enforcement and regulators with intelligence on techniques, trends, and patterns of suspected illicit activity within this market.

Of the filers who reported dollar amounts involved, the greatest concentration (45 percent), reported suspected fraud in transactions valued under $1 million.[3] Nine percent of transactions were valued at $10 million or more. Approximately half of CRE SARs named subjects located in five states: Georgia, Illinois, Florida, New York, and California.

Filers noted several different kinds of suspicious activity related to CRE fraud. The top four reported categories in order were: False Documents, Misappropriation of Funds, Collusion-Bank Insider, and False Statements.

---

*   Reference in this report to any specific commercial product, service, process, or enterprise, or the use of any commercial product or enterprise, trade, firm, or corporation name is for the information and convenience of the public, and does not constitute endorsement or recommendation by the Financial Crimes Enforcement Network. With respect to materials generated by entities outside of the Financial Crimes Enforcement Network, permission to use these materials, if necessary, must be obtained from the original source. The Financial Crimes Enforcement Network assumes no responsibility for the content or operation of other Web sites.

1. Congressional Oversight Panel, *February Oversight Report – Commercial Real Estate Losses and the Risk to Financial Stability*, Page 2, 10 February 2010 at http://cop.senate.gov/documents/cop-021110-report.pdf

2. Business Wire, "Fitch U.S. CMBS Newsletter: New Issuance Leads to Lower Delinquency Forecast of 10%," 7 January 2011 at http://www.businesswire.com/news/home/20110107005551/en/Fitch-U.S.-CMBS-Newsletter-Issuance-Leads-Delinquency

3. Statistics in this paragraph derive from the total average of SAR fillings from 2007 through 2010.

"False documents" included fraudulent rent rolls related to multi-family residential and commercial property, tax documentation, identification documents, appraisals, and forged signatures.[4] Filers reported subjects misappropriating funds in several ways, including diverting the proceeds of commercial loans to fund personal expenses or to support businesses facing insolvency.

Examples of fraud or illicit activity reported in SARs and described in this report include a case where a bank insider's suspicious client base allegedly moved with him from employer to employer.[5] Also described are examples where customers reportedly sold CRE collateral without disclosure to the lender, pledged the same collateral for multiple purposes, and hid or conveyed collateral to associates.

FinCEN will use this study, and other studies like it, to inform future rulemaking and to provide information that may be of value to financial institutions. Additionally, studies like this one further our ongoing efforts to support law enforcement in allocating resources and the investigation and prosecution of individual criminal cases. Making public this type of study helps banks and other financial institutions spot and report illicit activity to FinCEN that is useful to state, local and federal law enforcement and regulators.

---

4. Rent rolls are documents that state how much rent the property owners receive per unit. Filers reported numerous instances in which borrowers submitted inflated rent rolls to enhance their loan application.
5. For this study, the term bank insider refers to persons employed by the lending institution. In most instances, bank insiders were commercial lending officers.

Purpose

This report provides an overview of suspected fraud involving CRE financing, as reported in a sample of Bank Secrecy Act (BSA) SAR filings.[6] It is the latest in a series of publications issued by FinCEN regarding fraud and other illicit activities in the residential and CRE markets.[7]

The primary purpose of this report is to describe CRE fraud trends and patterns and to provide examples of suspicious activities within the context of the CRE market. FinCEN is publishing this report to aid in the detection and prevention of fraud and to help financial institutions identify the kinds of activities that may warrant SAR filings related to CRE fraud.

---

6. For purposes of this report, SAR refers only to the Suspicious Activity Report filed by depository institutions (TD F 90-22.47). Most CRE-related fraud occurs in the context of commercial loan transactions and related activities conducted by banks and other insured depository institutions. As such, this report does not address other types of SARs (*e.g.*, those filed by casinos, money services businesses, and the securities and futures industry).

7. FinCEN reports on mortgage fraud may be viewed on the FinCEN website at http://www.fincen.gov/mortgagefraud.html.

Background

The scope of the CRE market and the financing structure that underpins it are extensive. The CRE market includes brokerage and lending services for the industrial, retail, office, hotel, and multi-family housing sectors. SARs related to the CRE market involve a variety of transactions and activities related to the purchase and development of raw land as well as the acquisition, development, construction, and improvement of commercial buildings. Developers and other CRE-related businesses use commercial mortgages, construction loans, multi-family mortgages, and land loans to facilitate CRE activities. Borrowers also use CRE holdings as collateral for other types of commercial loans.

As commercial rents and occupancy rates have fallen and commercial loan defaults have risen over the last several years, concern has grown about the CRE market and its potential effects on the nation's economy.[8] In 2006, the FDIC published two reports foreshadowing problems within the CRE market.[9] One report indicated that insured institutions with CRE holdings in excess of 300 percent of total capital were beyond levels seen before the CRE crisis of the late 1980s.[10] The reports also signaled concerns over lax underwriting and the potential that unforeseen events could lower rents, reduce property values, and limit refinancing options.[11]

---

8. Lingling Wei, "CMBS Savior? Developers Diversified Deal Is Nearer," *Wall Street Journal*, 4 November 2009, Page C14; Michael Murray, "More than 1000 Banks Face CRE Loan Exposure," *MBA NewsLink*, at http://www.mortgagebankers.org/tools/FullStory.aspx?ArticleId=11356

9. FDIC, *Economic Conditions and Emerging Risks in Banking*, 9 May 2006 at http://www.fdic.gov/deposit/insurance/risk/2006_02/Economic_2006_02.html; FDIC, the Office of the Comptroller of the Currency, and the Board of Governors of the Federal Reserve System, *Joint Guidance: Concentration in CRE Lending, Sound Risk Management Practices*, December 2006 at http://www.fdic.gov/regulations/laws/federal/2006/06notice1212.html

10. FDIC, *Economic Conditions and Emerging Risks in Banking*, 9 May 2006 at http://www.fdic.gov/deposit/insurance/risk/2006_02/Economic_2006_02.html

11. See footnote 9.

Of key concern is the estimated $1.4 trillion in CRE loans that will reach the end of their terms between 2010 and 2014.[12] As the loans become due, analysts anticipate a delinquency rate of 10 percent because some borrowers will be unable to refinance their loans due either to stricter underwriting standards, or because the loan amounts outstanding exceed property values.[13] The valuation of the overall CRE market has fallen approximately 42 percent since it peaked in October 2007, with future fluctuation in CRE prices expected.[14]

---

12. Congressional Oversight Panel, *February Oversight Report – Commercial Real Estate Losses and the Risk to Financial Stability*, Page 2, 10 February 2010 at http://cop.senate.gov/documents/cop-021110-report.pdf

13. Business Wire, "Fitch U.S. CMBS Newsletter: New Issuance Leads to Lower Delinquency Forecast of 10%," 7 January 2011 at http://www.businesswire.com/news/home/20110107005551/en/Fitch-U.S.-CMBS-Newsletter-Issuance-Leads-Delinquency

14. Moody's Investors Service, *Moody's/REAL Commercial Property Price Indices*, December 2010 at http://www.realindices.com/pdf/CPPI_1210.pdf

Methodology

This assessment describes suspicious activities relating to the financing of commercial property as reported in depository institution SARs filed from January 1, 2007, through December 31, 2010.[15]

FinCEN analysts identified 1,596 depository institution SARs filed from 2007 through 2009 involving potential CRE fraud. As the SAR form does not include a checkbox for CRE fraud, analysts identified these potentially relevant reports by searching narratives of SARs with the Mortgage Loan Fraud or Commercial Loan Fraud characterizations of suspicious activity for terms related to CRE properties, financing, or uses.[16] Analysts then randomly sampled 310 of the 1,596 SARs for review.[17] Of the sampled SARs, 231 (75 percent) clearly involved CRE fraud.[18] Those 231 CRE fraud SARs were the basis for the 2007-2009 findings. The review showed that filers most commonly reported suspected CRE fraud using variations of the terms "commercial real estate," "commercial property," "commercial mortgage," and "construction loan" in SAR narratives.[19]

To provide the most recent data available, FinCEN duplicated this process by analyzing CRE fraud SAR filings from January 1, 2010, through December 31, 2010. Using this methodology, analysts identified 531 potential CRE fraud SARs filed in 2010. Analysts then generated a random sample of 244 SAR filings, of which 186 (76 percent) were CRE-related. The 186 relevant CRE fraud SARs were the basis for the 2010 findings.

Analysts then identified trends, patterns, and examples of activities described in the relevant sample SARs. FinCEN also researched government reports and information reported in the media about the CRE industry and legal proceedings related to subjects of the relevant sample SARs.

---

15. Analysts used the SAR filing date rather than the suspicious activity dates to compile the pool of SAR data for this report. Therefore, some activities described herein predate the January 1, 2007, filing date.

16. Initial analysis of BSA data containing CRE-related terms indicated that SARs with other characterizations of suspicious activity were generally not related to the financing of CRE.

17. The sample size of 310 SARs represents a 95 percent confidence level with +/- 5 percent variance.

18. Another 78 SARs (25 percent) were either inapplicable or of indeterminable relevance.

19. Filers used a variety of terms to describe CRE fraud-related activities, which posed a challenge for analysts trying to identify this type of activity within the BSA database. Analysts looked for numerous descriptive terms to identify potential CRE fraud, including "commercial property," "commercial real estate," and "commercial mortgage" in conjunction with "construction," "develop," "land," "industrial," "multi-family," "retail," and "office."

Research and Analysis

The following section provides an overview of CRE fraud SARs during calendar years 2007 through 2010. It covers annual filing totals, reported activities and transaction amounts, locations of subjects, and regulators of filing institutions.[20]

SAR Filings

CRE fraud SAR filings generally increased from 2007 through 2009 before peaking in the first quarter of 2010. Although filings decreased throughout 2010, they remained at levels higher than prior years.

GRAPH 1

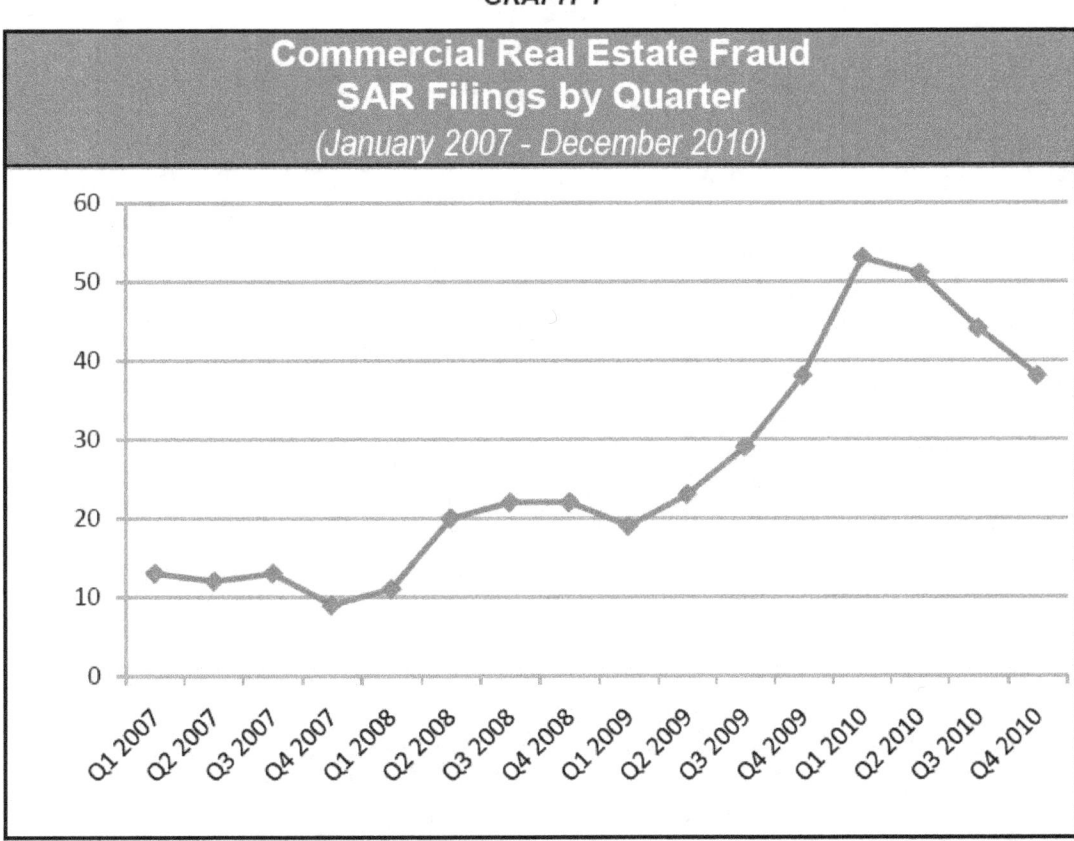

---

20. The statistics were based upon data from samples generated for years 2007-2009 and 2010. The 2007-2009 statistics are based upon 231 CRE-related sample SARs and the 2010 statistics are based on 186 CRE-related sample SARs (See Methodology Section.)

Increases in SAR filings are not necessarily indicative of an overall increase in CRE fraud activities over the same period, because financial institutions may not detect and report suspected CRE fraud until a later date.[21] The volume of SAR filings in any given period does not directly correlate to the number or timing of suspected fraudulent incidents in that period.

Research revealed 73 percent of the 2010 SARs originated from different financial institutions, indicating that CRE fraud affects a wide range of institutions from varying sizes and locations. Likewise, between 2007 and 2009 71 percent of SARs originated from different financial institutions. For all these years, the top filer submitted 6 percent of SARs. This filing pattern differs from the results learned in recent mortgage loan fraud studies showing that a relatively small number of filers submitted the majority of SARs.[22]

---

21. For an example of suspicious activity similar to CRE fraud explaining the lag between suspicious activity dates and filing dates, see FinCEN's March 2009 report, *Mortgage Loan Fraud Connections with Other Financial Crime: An Evaluation of Suspicious Activity Reports Filed by Money Services Businesses, Securities and Futures Firms, Insurance Companies and Casinos*, at http://www.fincen.gov/news_room/rp/files/mortgage_fraud.pdf

22. FinCEN, *Filing Trends in Mortgage Loan Fraud*, February 2009 at http://www.fincen.gov/news_room/nr/pdf/20090225a.pdf

Time Range of Filings

The following table represents the length of time between when the suspicious activity ended and when the filer submitted the SAR.[23] Filers submitted over 40 percent of SARs within 30 days of the suspicious activity end date.

TABLE 1

Commercial Real Estate Fraud SARs Time Elapsed: Suspicious Activity End Date to Reporting Date[24] (January 2007 - December 2010)		
Time Elapsed	**2007-2009 SARs[25]**	**2010 SARs**
No End Date Reported	6%	5%
< 30 days	46%	44%
30 < 60 days	13%	13%
60 < 90 days	8%	7%
90 < 180 days	6%	11%
180 < 365 days	9%	7%
1 < 2 years	8%	5%
2 + years	5%	8%

Characterizations of Suspicious Activity

The SAR form does not have a separate checkbox for CRE fraud. Filers differentiated CRE fraud from residential mortgage loan fraud by selecting the Commercial Loan Fraud characterization checkbox of suspicious activity categories in almost all CRE fraud SARs. As noted in the Methodology section, all data derived from term searches of SARs characterized as Commercial Loan Fraud and Mortgage Loan Fraud. These are 2 of the 21 checkboxes in Field 35 on the SAR form.[26] Filers also used a variety of narrative terms to describe suspected CRE fraud. Some of these terms, and the activities they describe, are the same as those used to describe residential mortgage

---

23. The suspicious activity end date reported in Part III, Field 33 of the SAR form (TD F 90-22.47) might not always be the detection date of the suspicious activity. See "When Does the 30-Day Time Period in which to File a Suspicious Activity Report Begin?" *The SAR Activity Review-Trends, Tips & Issues,* Issue 10, May 2006 at http://www.fincen.gov/news_room/rp/files/sar_tti_10.pdf

24. Data derived from Part IV, Field 50 (TD F 90-22.47).

25. Due to rounding, percentages do not total 100 percent.

26. See FinCEN, *Suspicious Activity Report* at http://www.fincen.gov/forms/files/f9022-47_sar-di.pdf

fraud. However, other terms identified in the SARs, such as "commercial real estate," "commercial property," "commercial mortgage," and "construction loan," are more specific to the commercial real estate market.

Filers may check more than one box for characterization of suspicious activity in a single SAR. In addition to Commercial Loan Fraud or Mortgage Loan Fraud, filers checked False Statement as an additional activity in 30 percent of 2010 SARs. Similarly, FinCEN mortgage loan fraud reports indicate that filers consistently select False Statement in approximately one quarter of SARs involving suspected Mortgage Loan Fraud.[27]

In 2010, the selection of Other almost doubled in percentage points from the 2007-2009 data. Filers commonly used Other to provide additional description about activities, including misappropriation of funds, appraisal fraud, forgery, and conveyance of collateral.

SAR Narratives

Analysis of the 2010 SAR narratives revealed similar activity types reported in preceding years, with minor shifts in reporting levels. The number of SAR narratives describing the use of false documentation increased nine percentage points over the previous period. The increase was especially apparent in the reporting of forged signatures. Narrative analysis also revealed a significant increase in non-disclosure of information to lenders, which impacted banks' lending decisions.

TABLE 2

Commercial Real Estate Fraud SARs Top Five Activities Described in Narratives (January 2007 - December 2010)[28]		
Activity	**2007-2009 SARs**	**2010 SARs**
False Documents	42%	51%
Misappropriation of Funds	29%	27%
Bank Insider Collusion	19%	13%
False Statements	15%	10%
Non-Disclosure to Lender	9%	19%

27. The report included 15,697 mortgage loan fraud SARs, of which 4,144 indicated the additional activity of "False Statement" (26 percent). See FinCEN, *Mortgage Loan Fraud Update*, February 2010 at http://www.fincen.gov/news_room/rp/files/MLF_Update.pdf

28. Some filers reported multiple types of suspicious activities within one SAR narrative. Therefore, percentages exceed 100 percent.

Filers most commonly cited misrepresentations involving documentation, false statements, misappropriation of funds, and collusion involving bank insiders as suspicious activities. Filers reported the following suspicious activities.

False Documents:

Filers most commonly cited suspected misrepresentations involving documentation. Common misrepresentations included fraudulent rent rolls, tax documentation, financial statements, identification documents, appraisals, and forged signatures. Filers suspected that bank insiders sometimes colluded by providing false documents to loan approval committees, approving loan disbursements after reviewing fraudulent invoices, and submitting incomplete paperwork. Additional activities included false claims of property ownership.

Misappropriation of Funds:

Filers suspected misappropriation of funds in nearly 30 percent of CRE fraud SARs for the entire review period, indicating diversion of funds for personal profit or support to businesses facing insolvency. Filers discovered the suspicious activity after learning that borrowers filed for bankruptcy or after finding undisclosed liens on collateral, fraudulent disbursement documentation, and/or inspecting sites with little or no construction work performed. Roughly half the SARs describing misappropriation of funds were for transactions under $1 million.

Bank Insider Collusion:

Filers described possible collusion with borrowers and real estate insiders. In these situations, a bank insider's role in collusion was essential to facilitating the loan approval process and funds disbursement. In most suspected instances of bank insider collusion, filers referenced false documents and the misappropriation of funds.

Non-Disclosure to Lender:

Filers reported that borrowers did not disclose key information to lenders thereby affecting lending decisions. A common example was non-disclosure of debt, such as a mortgage, on financial statements. Many filers stated they would have denied the loan applications if they had known of the debts. Additionally, borrowers did not inform lenders when they sold or transferred properties or engaged in side agreements with property buyers.

Suspicious Activity Amounts

Although some filers reported the entire transaction amount in the suspicious activity amount field (Part III, Field 34) of the SAR, others reported only the portion of the amount they considered suspicious. For instance, in the case of participation loans, some filers reported the amount of the whole loan while other filers reported only their portion of the participation amount.[29]

Analysis of all CRE fraud SARs showed that the largest class of suspicious transactions, roughly 45 percent, were under one million dollars.

TABLE 3

Commercial Real Estate Fraud SARs Transaction Amount Range (January 2007 - December 2010)		
SAR Amount in Millions	**2007-2009 SARs[30]**	**2010 SARs**
(Blank)	4%	3%
< $1	44%	46%
$1 < $2	16%	15%
$2 < $3	7%	7%
$3 < $4	4%	6%
$4 < $5	7%	3%
$5 < $6	2%	4%
$6 < $7	2%	3%
$7 < $8	1%	3%
$8 < $9	2%	1%
$9 < $10	1%	1%
$10 +	9%	8%

29. FinCEN understands a participation loan to mean a collaboration among lenders to share interest or ownership in a loan or a package of loans where one of the participants, called the lead bank or lead lender, services the loan. Participation loans make it possible for large borrowers to obtain bank financing when the amount involved exceeds the lending limit of an individual bank.

30. Due to rounding, percentages do not total 100 percent.

TABLE 4

Commercial Real Estate Fraud SARs Transaction Amounts Under $1 Million (January 2007 - December 2010)		
SAR Amount	**2007-2009 SARs**	**2010 SARs**
< $100,000	7%	6%
$100,000 < $200,000	10%	6%
$200,000 < $500,000	12%	19%
$500,000 < $1,000,000	15%	15%

Filer Branch Locations

Georgia, Illinois, and California were the top filer branch locations in 2010, representing 24 percent of CRE fraud SAR filings. Texas was previously a top filer based on the 2007-2009 data, but its filings decreased significantly in 2010.

Subject Locations

Analysis of the 2007-2009 and the 2010 CRE fraud SARs revealed the same top subject locations.

TABLE 5

Commercial Real Estate Fraud SARs Top Five Filings by Subject Location (January 2007 - December 2010)		
Subject Location	**2007-2009 SARs**	**2010 SARs**
Georgia	12%	10%
Illinois	11%	9%
Florida	10%	8%
New York	9%	11%
California	8%	8%

These locations correlated directly with locations for subjects reported in mortgage loan fraud SARs.[31] Direct correlations between branch and subject locations did not exist, because subjects often obtained interstate financing. For instance, in 2010 New York filers submitted only six of the SARs, but 48 subjects had New York addresses.

---

31. See FinCEN, *Mortgage Loan Fraud: An Update of Trends based Upon an Analysis of Suspicious Activity Reports*, April 2008 at http://www.fincen.gov/news_room/rp/files/MortgageLoanFraudSARAssessment.pdf

Suspicious Activity Examples

The following section provides examples of suspected CRE fraud involving commercial property, including land, condominiums, office buildings, stores, hotels, and single-family homes. The subjects of these activities include bank insiders, real estate industry insiders, construction companies, and commercial loan borrowers. An overview of the most commonly cited forms of suspicious activity from 2007 through 2010 follows.

Misrepresentations: Subjects allegedly made false statements and/or submitted falsified documents including rent rolls, tax documentation, appraisals, draw requests, lien waivers, and financial statements to bolster loan applications.[32] Filers also reported that subjects made fraudulent disbursement requests, including fraudulent invoices and receipts, to receive loan proceeds. Additionally, filers reported that some subjects used similar scams to defraud multiple banks.

Misappropriation of Funds: Filers reported that borrowers potentially misappropriated funds by diverting them to other projects. The activity was discovered when the borrowers filed for bankruptcy or when filers performed site inspections.

Bank Insider Collusion: Filers suspected fraud when bank insiders breached multiple bank policies and procedures. Filers described possible collusion with borrowers and/ or real estate insiders. Bank insiders reportedly played essential roles in facilitating the loan approval process and disbursing funds. In several instances, filers indicated that bank insiders' suspicious client bases moved with them from employer to employer.

---

32. "Appraisal fraud is usually [intentional] fraud or negligence on the part of the appraiser, often in collusion with other parties. Some institutions have internal appraisers, but most use outside companies. Manipulating or inflating ... market values and property characteristics are tactics of appraisal fraud. ... Appraisal fraud can be used to qualify an undervalued [property] for a higher mortgage amount (usually fraud for property) or to inflate the value of real estate so that the property can be resold or flipped quickly to a straw or duped buyer and the profit retained by perpetrators (fraud for profit) ... Mortgage brokers or loan officers [may pressure appraisers] to falsify an appraisal so that a loan transaction can be approved, [or an] appraiser [may work] in collusion with other conspirators to perpetrate the fraud." See FDIC, "Staying Alert to Mortgage Fraud," *Supervisory Insights*, Summer 2007 at http://www.fdic.gov/regulations/examinations/supervisory/insights/sisum07/sisum07.pdf

<u>Flipping [33] and Straw Buyer Schemes:</u> Filers described schemes involving flipping and straw buyers to generate equity for another purchase, for profit, and to improve borrowers' creditworthiness.

<u>Collateral Transfer:</u> Filers described instances where borrowers possibly sold collateral without disclosure to the lender, did not forward proceeds of collateral sales to the lenders, hid or conveyed the collateral to associates, or quit-claim deeded [34] the collateral to another entity. Several examples involved transfers of ownership to family members or trust accounts. Filers described instances in which borrowers' actions, such as diverting funds for collateral improvements to other projects or inflating collateral values, negatively affected the banks' financial positions.

<u>Advance Fee Schemes:</u> Filers described various forms of advance fee schemes targeting borrowers, lenders, and companies unable to obtain CRE financing. These schemes involved fraudulent business proposals and financial instruments.

<u>Other Suspicious Activities:</u> Filers reported suspicious activities involving money laundering and structuring as well as insurance fraud.

---

33. Flipping is the practice of generating a profit by buying and selling a property multiple times within a short period. Although flipping is legal, numerous illegal flipping schemes use appraisers to inflate property values and straw buyers to purchase the properties. For instance, suppose a fraudster paid $1 million for a property. The next day he used a false appraisal to establish a higher property value and worked with a straw buyer who received a loan for $2 million to purchase that property. The fraudster would profit by pocketing the excess loan proceeds or investing them as equity in further transactions. In executing flipping schemes, fraudsters may employ aliases to conceal the connection between the buyer and seller. They may also submit to the lender false and misleading financial statements and documents.

34. A quit-claim deed conveys any interest one may have in a property to another party. It does not warrant that the property is free from any liens, nor does it provide other assurances found in the more common general warranty deed. In a general warranty deed, the seller guarantees that he or she owns the property and is conveying it to the buyer with a title that is free and clear, with the exception of any liens, encumbrances, or similar rights described in the title documents.

Misrepresentations

Filers commonly reported suspected misrepresentations in financial statements, tax documents, rent rolls, draw requests, and lien waivers.

<u>False Documents</u>

- Stock Manipulation

Filers reported that employees of a general contracting company allegedly inflated the company's stock price before an executive sold millions of dollars in company shares. One employee allegedly engaged in a separate revenue-inflation scheme by booking fake construction revenue from undisclosed contracts with entities he controlled, causing the firm to record profits for little work performed. This inflated revenue helped to increase the stock price, and the executive sold millions of dollars in stock when the price peaked.

A SAR filer reported that a company materially misstated financial documents to qualify for funding. A company executive allegedly used his position to make project commitments and construction loan guarantees to his related business interests. The filer cited questionable accounting records, which it used as a key determinant of the borrower's creditworthiness. The filer's loan was part of a large participation and syndication loan involving other financial institutions. The bank expected to lose several million dollars.

- Rent Rolls

Many filers cited suspected fraudulent rent rolls as a form of false documentation to facilitate the approval of a CRE loan. Banks typically discovered discrepancies after property inspections and denied the loan requests.

One filer reported that a property owner attempted to refinance multiple loans for millions of dollars by misrepresenting rent rolls to inflate his income. An appraiser visited the properties and confirmed with the property manager that the correct rent rolls were significantly lower than the borrower had stated. The bank denied the application due to insufficient income. According to another SAR, a subject allegedly stated he based the rent rolls on projections for future growth. A filer also described a borrower's accusation that a mortgage broker forged his signature on rent rolls.

- Draw Requests

A filer reported that a borrower potentially misrepresented the draw requests on its construction loan to renovate a multi-unit apartment complex. The borrower depleted the loan funds less than halfway through the project, prompting a bank review. The filer reported draw requests based on dissimilar invoices from the same company, receipts dated prior to the loan, receipts from stores not affiliated with construction, and financial statements in lieu of invoices.

- Forged Cancellation of Deed of Trust

A filer reported that a borrower allegedly provided a forged cancellation of another bank's deed of trust to obtain CRE financing. When the borrower later filed for bankruptcy, the bank discovered the cancellation was a forgery.

- Factoring

Factoring is a transaction whereby a business sells its accounts receivable to a third party at a discounted rate to receive funds to finance its business operations. Fraudsters may use phony documents, such as statements of accounts receivable, to exploit and obtain funds from factoring businesses.

For example, a filer reported a borrower received approval for a revolving loan facility[35] to fund a factoring business based upon the borrower's fraudulent accounts receivable statements, which included a purported construction contract. Another filer reported that a borrower with a revolving loan facility discovered its factoring division had millions of dollars of fraudulent accounts receivable from various industries, including construction companies.

False Statements

- Bid Rigging

Filers reported on subjects, subsequently indicted on multiple charges, for involvement in a bid-rigging fraud conspiracy related to contracts for the investment of municipal bond proceeds to fund affordable housing.[36] Public entities that issue municipal bonds hired the subjects as their broker to conduct a competitive bidding process for contracts to invest proceeds from municipal bond issuance. The subjects

---

35. A revolving loan facility is an arrangement that enables the borrower to withdraw, repay, and redraw loan funds within a set period.

36. The SARs referenced in this section were not included in the study sample, but the connection between CRE fraud and affordable housing warrants mention.

allegedly manipulated the competitive bidding process for enrichment by sharing information about pricing with co-conspirators as well as intentionally submitting losing bids. The subjects had ties to a real estate development company, an advisory firm specializing in reinvestment of municipal bonds, and affordable housing projects.

- False Claim of Forgery

A filer reported that a contractor defaulted on a small number of construction loans. As the bank began the foreclosure process, the contractor claimed that the other guarantor forged his signature on the loan guarantee. The bank suspected the contractor's claim was false and an attempt to avoid liability for the loan guarantees.

Non-Disclosure – Transfer of CRE

A filer reported that borrowers transferred their real estate holdings from their personal names to a living trust without disclosing this information to the lender, thus impairing the personal guarantees they presented to the bank. The borrowers had a construction loan to build town homes and an acquisition loan to purchase lots.

Misappropriation of Funds

Filers regularly reported misappropriation of funds in which borrowers diverted funds for profit, personal use, and business solvency. Filers often learned of this activity when they conducted site inspections or when mechanics' liens appeared on their collateral.

Multiple Lenders Defrauded

A filer reported that a builder, subsequently convicted of bank fraud against multiple banks, used false documentation to misappropriate funds from multiple construction loans. The bank suspected the borrower falsified draw requests and forged lien waivers in order to receive multiple loan advances. On touring the properties, bank personnel saw no construction on the lots.

Commingling Funds

A filer reported that a borrower misappropriated funds from a construction loan to build a residential home before declaring bankruptcy. The loan agreement approved the funding of a building permit and a lot purchase. The borrower allegedly never obtained a construction permit for the project, and instead presented another property's permit to the bank. The bank suspected that the borrower commingled funds with another building project not financed by the bank.

Bank Insiders

Filers commonly referenced bank insiders involved in violations of bank lending policies, collusion, fraudulent inspections, inappropriate paperwork and disbursements, misleading loan approval committees, approvals of non-creditworthy clients, and unauthorized loans and collateral waivers. According to filers, subjects carried out these activities due to negligence, to maintain or enhance their reputations, or for money. Several filers reported that bank insiders moved from bank to bank with their suspicious client base.

Suspicious Client Base

A filer suspected a bank insider of colluding with real estate insiders and clients who moved with him to several different banks. Subjects included the bank insider, the appraiser, borrowers and related entities, and a realty company. The bank insider had a portfolio consisting of hundreds of loans, mostly for multi-family properties worth over $300 million. The banker originated dozens of improvement loans exceeding $100 million. One borrower received a mortgage loan to acquire and improve a property after a fire. However, a site inspection revealed the property was boarded up, abandoned, and valued at less than a quarter of the loan amount. A review of loan records revealed multiple lien waivers for the same improvements, missing dates and signatures, suspect rent rolls, proceeds converted to cash in round numbers, and debits under $10,000.

Hotel-Condominium Conversion Scheme

A filer reported a hotel-condominium conversion scheme involving suspected collusion among a senior lending officer, a developer, and a financier that led to millions of dollars in defaulted loans, which contributed to a bank failure and a foreclosure on a hotel that provided half the city's tax revenue.[37] Suspicious activity included inconsistencies in how the bank insider presented, processed, and funded the loan; collateral inconsistencies; and collusion. The filer cited an alleged conspiracy to mislead lenders or investors into extending credit or capital based on an inflated purchase price.

---

37. A condominium-hotel conversion occurs when a property owner sells a hotel to retail investors but the property continues to operate as a hotel. Room investors can stay at the property, but the room is rented when they check out. This scenario differs from hotels that are purchased to become only condominiums.

Fee Generation

A filer suspected collusion by a bank insider to receive loan proceeds from a borrower who followed the insider from another bank to obtain refinancing. The insider orchestrated a series of small loan increases to the borrower after which the borrower issued checks to a company that the bank insider apparently owned.

Collusion

Filers reported many instances of alleged collusion involving buyers, sellers, developers, construction companies, and real estate professionals such as appraisers, mortgage brokers, and title companies. Filers described schemes involving flipping and straw buyers to generate equity for another purchase, profit, or to improve borrowers' creditworthiness.

Flipping

- Generate Profit and Equity

A filer reported that a seller flipped a multi-tenant retail and office building to enable the buyer to avoid using his own funds in the transaction. As part of this transaction, the seller sold a shopping center to a buyer for several million dollars. On the same day, the buyer flipped the property to an affiliate of the original seller for an inflated appraised value. The relationship between the buyers and seller was not disclosed to the lender. By flipping the property for a profit, the borrower avoided using his own funds for the 25 percent equity stake in the property, which later foreclosed.

- Side Agreements[38]

A filer was a participant with other banks in a construction and development loan for a luxury condominium building. The filing bank later learned that the unit buyers executed "side agreements" with the developer in violation of the bank's loan agreement. The borrower advised the bank he allegedly had multiple "accommodation agreements" for units that investors purchased but would not close. He thought the buyers would be able to flip/resell their units prior to the closing date and expected several non-investor purchases to close. Eventually the developer admitted he had inadequate funding to finish the project.

---

38. In this example, the "side agreements" included a discount on the purchase price, an accommodation payment, and termination of the "purchase and sale agreement."

<u>Straw Buyer Schemes</u>

Straw buyer schemes commonly utilize qualified or fraudulently qualified borrowers to receive loans and then transfer ownership of the collateral asset and/or the proceeds of the loan to another entity, often for payment. This transfer of ownership usually occurs without the bank's knowledge. SAR filers often reported that straw buyers were complicit and paid for their participation in such schemes. However, one filer described a CRE developer that used unwitting straw buyers under the guise of an investment opportunity.

- Straw Buyer – Ownership Transfer

A filer reported that its customer possibly used his limited liability company (LLC) as a straw buyer that received a multi-million dollar loan for an office building after the bank denied his associates a loan because of adverse background checks. The LLC owned 100 percent of the denied borrowers' company, the operating entity for the building. The bank also issued a commercial line of credit to cover bond issues that the entity was assuming from the previous owners. In settlement discussions after the loan defaulted, the borrower admitted he sold his ownership interest in the LLC to the denied borrowers and failed to notify the bank, contrary to the loan agreement.

- Bank Fraud Scheme – Mortgage Brokers and Straw Buyers

A filer reported that a subject, subsequently indicted on multiple charges, defrauded banks out of millions of dollars by colluding with straw buyers and mortgage brokerage companies. Another bank alerted the filer to potential fraud involving several banks and numerous commercial loans. The same straw buyer signed multiple pre-sale contracts, and the same mortgage company prequalified the buyer. The subject pre-sold homes and acquired funding for their construction. Eventually the subject defaulted on a loan and abandoned the job site.

- Duped Straw Buyer

A filer reported that a property development company purchased numerous lots in a subdivision and allegedly used straw buyers to flip the lots at inflated prices by paying them fees, promising to make their loan payments, and agreeing to repurchase the lots within a year. However, the developer made no loan payments. One of the straw buyers contacted the bank to advise she was unable to make the loan payments herself and claimed that the developer advised her to lie about her employment and income on the loan application.

Collateral Transfer

Filers described instances where borrowers possibly sold, hid, or conveyed collateral, including transfers of ownership to family members, contrary to financing arrangements.

Sold Assets to Fund Purchase

A mobile home construction company, subsequently named in a consumer protection lawsuit, allegedly accepted thousands of dollars in consumer payments for mobile homes and services it did not provide, which prevented consumers from taking legal title to the homes. A filer reported that these subjects sold homes that served as collateral backing a line of credit without applying the sales proceeds to reduce the loan principal.

Sold Assets to Family Members

A filer reported that husband and wife business owners obtained a commercial line of credit and then sold the collateral to family members. First liens on all assets of their two companies and second real estate mortgages on multiple rental properties served as collateral. The bank later renewed and converted the line of credit to a term commercial loan. The borrowers became delinquent on payments and filed for bankruptcy. During bankruptcy proceedings, the bank learned that at the time of the loan conversion, the borrowers failed to disclose that they had dissolved the operations of the businesses and sold the business assets to other family members.

Hid Collateral

A filer reported that borrowers with several delinquent loans for CRE, residential property, and equipment transferred collateral to avoid obligations to creditors and evade taxes. The borrowers filed for bankruptcy and allegedly hid equipment that served as collateral for their loans at an employee's home and at a family member's business.

Advance Fee Schemes

Filers described various forms of advance fee schemes targeting borrowers, lenders, and companies unable to obtain CRE financing. These schemes involved fraudulent business proposals and financial instruments. Some of these activities directly involved financing through a bank.

CRE Developers As Victims

A filer reported that an individual generated over a million dollars in an advance fee scheme by targeting CRE developers unable to secure financing during the economic downturn. For a large fee, he offered to raise financing for their projects. However, he allegedly never provided financing, and the victims lost their fees. He had also claimed to give a portion of the fees associated with the loans to charities, but the filer did not detect any account activity consistent with funding real estate mortgages or charity donations.

Suspicious Proposal

A filer reported that a group of business associates proposed a scheme in which the bank would purchase U.S. Treasury Bonds and in return receive a letter of credit to finance a large commercial property. The bank recognized the proposal as a potential scam and ceased communications with the group.

Another filer reported a request from a broker for a high-dollar loan using properties located outside the United States as collateral to fund various factories. The bank was unable to confirm that the subject owned the properties and believed the request was fraudulent due to inconsistencies in the information provided.

Loan Modification Scam

A filer reported that its customer attempted to modify his commercial mortgage through a servicing company that was perpetrating an advance fee scheme. The bank advised the customer it was a scam when the customer stated that the company would only accept payment sent through a money transmitter.

Debt Elimination Scam

Reported debt elimination scams involved fraudulent promissory notes and checks from the U.S. Department of the Treasury and a Federal Reserve Bank. For example, a filer reported a potential debt elimination scam in which it received a "bonded promissory note" for a customer's CRE loans with directions to present it to the "FRB NYC." The bank informed the borrower the document was fraudulent and advised the borrower to contact law enforcement. The perpetrator of the scam is currently incarcerated and allegedly still operating debt elimination scams by convincing borrowers that the U.S. government establishes accounts for all citizens at birth and that the "bonded promissory note" allows them to access those funds.

Another filer reported that a borrower presented fraudulent "U.S. Department of the Treasury checks" to pay off multiple mortgages on investment properties. The customer aroused the bank's suspicion by giving very precise instructions for processing the checks through a particular office of the IRS, which he claimed was the clearinghouse of a trust from his family. The bank confirmed with the Department of the Treasury and the United States Secret Service that the checks were fraudulent and reported the incident to local police.

Other Suspicious Activities

<u>BSA Violations</u>

A filer reported that its borrower, a real estate developer and investor, conducted excessive—and possibly structured—cash transactions. The filer also stated the manner of the deposits and outgoing wire transfers indicated potential layering of transactions, because they often occurred between the accounts of the borrower and his retail business. Further, the bank received many questionable payments by third parties to the borrower's multiple CRE loans.

<u>Insurance Fraud</u>

A filer suspected its customer of committing insurance fraud by improperly cashing insurance checks issued for repairs to the collateral securing a CRE loan. The customer did not initially notify the bank of the damage to its collateral and cashed the insurance checks without obtaining the bank's required endorsement. When questioned by the bank, the customer refused to provide documentation and proof of the repairs made to the collateral. The bank alleged further that the customer attempted to improperly influence the insurance company into removing the bank as a payee on one check.

Next Steps

FinCEN views its efforts to analyze and address a wide range of fraud issues as a priority. We will continue to analyze the valuable BSA data reported by financial institutions to explore various aspects of fraud and other illicit activities in the residential and CRE markets, including possible ties with other criminal activity. We will also continue to work closely with federal and state regulatory partners; federal, state, and local law enforcement agencies; and international partners in coordinated efforts to combat fraud and promote financial stability.

Appendix – CRE Fraud Reported in SARs from 2007 through 2009

Overview

The following section provides an overview of CRE fraud SARs during calendar years 2007 through 2009. It covers annual filing totals, reported activities and transaction amounts, locations of subjects, and regulators of filing institutions. All figures and statistics in this section derive from the relevant 231 sample CRE fraud SARs.

Annual Filings from 2007 through 2009

CRE fraud SAR filings significantly increased from 2007 to 2009. Filers submitted nearly half of all CRE fraud SARs in 2009.

TABLE A1

Commercial Real Estate Fraud SARs Annual Breakdown SARs filed from January 2007 - December 2009	
Year	SARs[39]
2007	20%
2008	32%
2009	47%

However, not all the reported activity occurred during the year institutions filed the SARs. Based on the dates and duration of the suspicious activity reported in each SAR, the majority of reported activities took place from 2007 through 2008.

---

39. Due to rounding, percentages do not total 100 percent.

TABLE A2

Commercial Real Estate Fraud SARs Activity Dates[40] (January 2007 - December 2009)	
Year	**SARs[41]**
< 2007	14%
2007	53%
2008	55%
2009	32%

Time Range of Filings

The following table represents the length of time between when the suspicious activity ended and when the filer submitted the SAR.[42] Filers submitted 46 percent of SARs within 30 days after the suspicious activity ended.

TABLE A3

Commercial Real Estate Fraud SARs Time Elapsed: Suspicious Activity End Date to Reporting Date[43] (January 2007 - December 2009)	
Time Elapsed	**SARs[44]**
No End Date Reported	6%
< 30 days	46%
30 < 60 days	13%
60 < 90 days	8%
90 < 180 days	6%
180 < 365 days	9%
1 < 2 years	8%
2 + years	5%

40. Data derived from Part III, Field 33 (TD F 90-22.47).

41. Suspicious activity dates span more than one year in some instances. Therefore, percentages exceed 100 percent.

42. The suspicious activity end date reported in Part III, Field 33 of the SAR form (TD F 90-22.47) might not always be the detection date of the suspicious activity. See "When Does the 30-Day Time Period in which to File a Suspicious Activity Report Begin?" *The SAR Activity Review-Trends, Tips & Issues*, Issue 10, May 2006 at http://www.fincen.gov/news_room/rp/files/sar_tti_10.pdf

43. Data derived from Part IV, Field 50 (TD F 90-22.47).

44. Due to rounding, percentages do not total 100 percent.

A total of 163 different filing institutions, of varying sizes and locations, submitted the relevant 231 sample SARs, signaling that CRE fraud might affect a broad range of reporting entities. The top filer submitted 6 percent of these reports, and the top five filers represented only 14 percent of SARs filed. This filing pattern differs from the results learned from a 2009 mortgage loan fraud study showing that a relatively small number of top filers submitted the majority of SARs.[45]

Characterizations of Suspicious Activity

Filers differentiated CRE fraud from residential mortgage loan fraud by selecting the Commercial Loan Fraud characterization checkbox of suspicious activity categories in 97 percent of CRE fraud SARs. As noted in the Methodology section, all data derived from term searches of SARs characterized as Commercial Loan Fraud and Mortgage Loan Fraud. These are 2 of the 21 checkboxes in Field 35 on the SAR form.[46]

Filers may check more than one box for characterization of suspicious activity in a single SAR. In addition to Commercial Loan Fraud or Mortgage Loan Fraud, filers checked False Statement as an additional activity in 26 percent of SARs. FinCEN's 2009 mortgage loan fraud report also indicated that filers selected False Statement in 26 percent of SARs.[47]

---

45. FinCEN, *Filing Trends in Mortgage Loan Fraud*, February 2009 at http://www.fincen.gov/news_room/nr/pdf/20090225a.pdf

46. See FinCEN, *Suspicious Activity Report* at http://www.fincen.gov/forms/files/f9022-47_sar-di.pdf

47. The report included 15,697 mortgage loan fraud SARs, of which 4,144 indicated the additional activity of "False Statement" (26 percent). See FinCEN, *Mortgage Loan Fraud Update*, February 2010 at http://www.fincen.gov/news_room/rp/files/MLF_Update.pdf

---

GRAPH A1

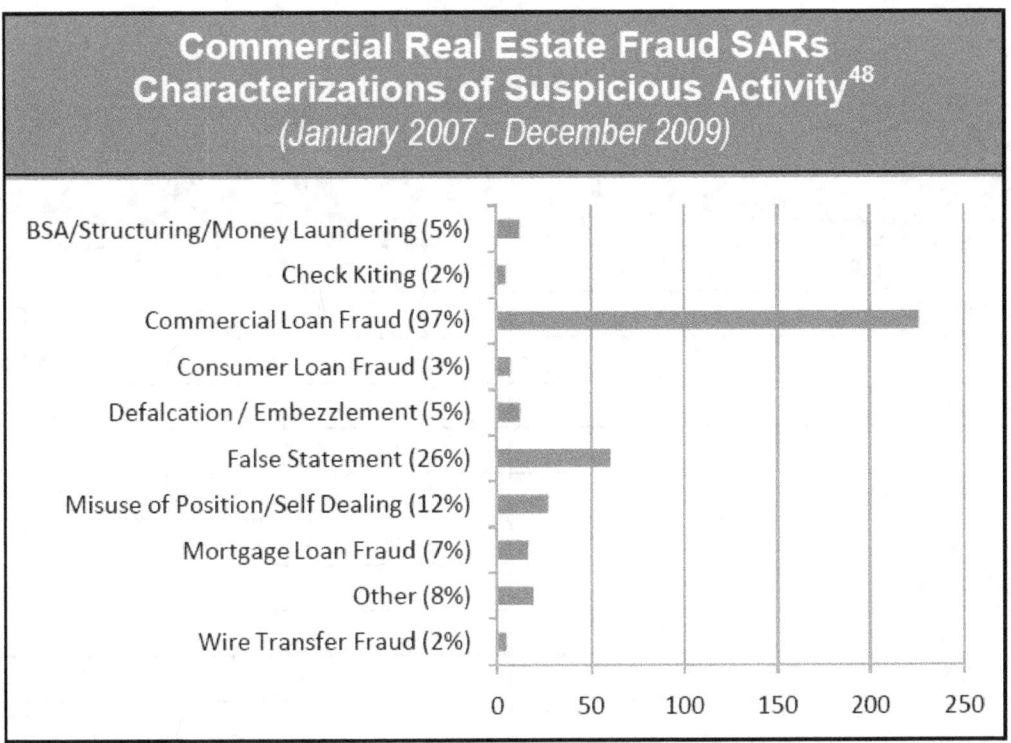

Commercial Real Estate Fraud SARs
Characterizations of Suspicious Activity[48]
(January 2007 - December 2009)

Suspicious Activity Amounts

While some filers reported the entire transaction amount in the suspicious activity amount field (Part III Field 34) of the SAR, others reported only the portion of the amount they considered suspicious For instance, in the case of participation loans, some filers reported the amount of the whole loan while other filers reported only their portion of the parti ipation amount.

---

48. Filers reported more than one characterization of suspicious activity in some SARs. Therefore, percentages exceed 100 percent.

The highest concentration of SARs (44 percent) referenced activity amounts under $1 million.

TABLE A4

Commercial Real Estate Fraud SARs Transaction Amount Range (January 2007 - December 2009)	
SAR Amount in Millions	**SARs[49]**
(Blank)	4%
< $1	44%
$1 < $2	16%
$2 < $3	7%
$3 < $4	4%
$4 < $5	7%
$5 < $6	2%
$6 < $7	2%
$7 < $8	1%
$8 < $9	2%
$9 < $10	1%
$10+	9%

Filer Branch and Subject Locations[50]

The following graphical maps show locations of suspected CRE fraud by filer branch and subject address.[51] Graph A2 indicates that the majority of filings for suspected CRE fraud came from Texas (9 percent); Georgia, Illinois, and California (7 percent each); and Michigan and Florida (6 percent each). Filers in these states submitted 42 percent of SARs.

The average CRE fraud SAR named more than three subjects. As shown in Graph A3, the majority of subjects in CRE fraud SARs were from Georgia (12 percent), Illinois (11 percent), Florida (10 percent), New York (9 percent), California (8 percent), and Texas (7 percent). Filers in these states submitted 57 percent of relevant SARs. These locations correlated directly with locations for subjects reported in mortgage loan fraud SARs.[52] Direct correlations between branch and subject locations did not

---

49. Due to rounding, percentages do not total 100 percent.

50. Maps also include SAR filings for the District of Columbia.

51. Although the maps depict filer branch and subject locations, the suspicious activity may have taken place in another state.

52. See FinCEN, *Mortgage Loan Fraud: An Update of Trends based Upon an Analysis of Suspicious Activity Reports*, April 2008 at http://www.fincen.gov/news_room/rp/files/MortgageLoanFraudSARAssessment.pdf

exist, as subjects often obtained interstate financing. For instance, New York filers submitted only six of the SARs, but 64 subjects had New York addresses.

GRAPH A2

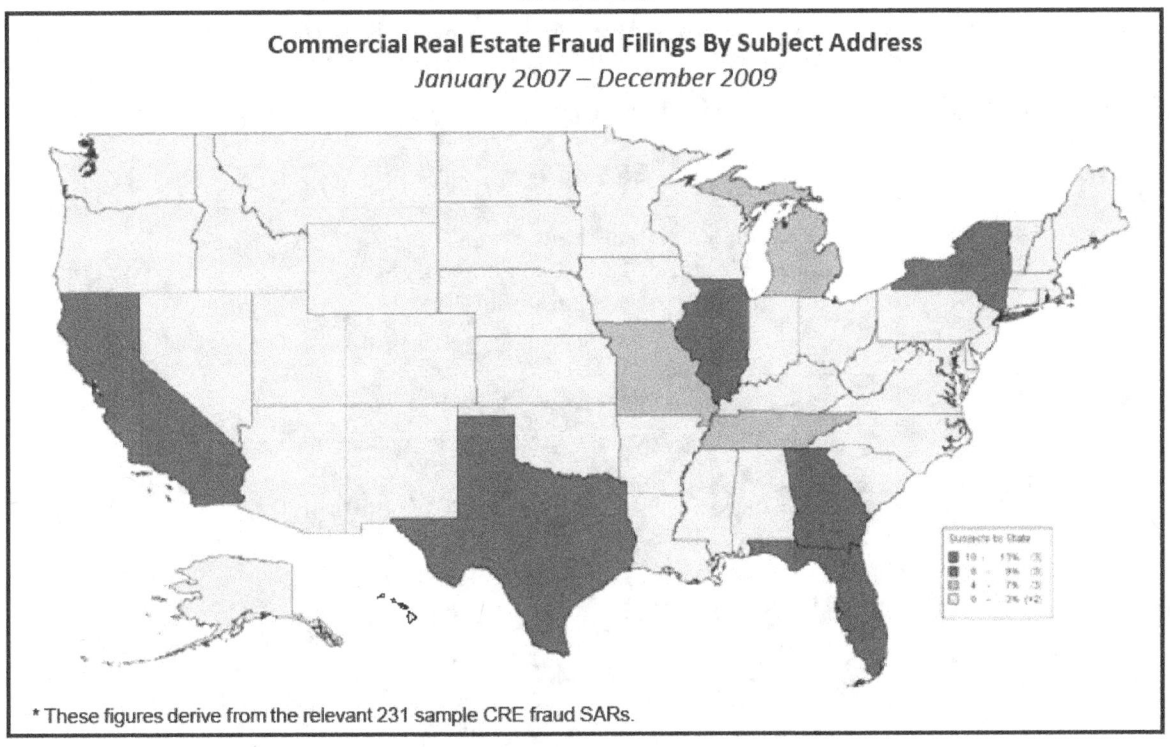

Commercial Real Estate Fraud Filings By Subject Address
January 2007 – December 2009

* These figures derive from the relevant 231 sample CRE fraud SARs.

GRAPH A3

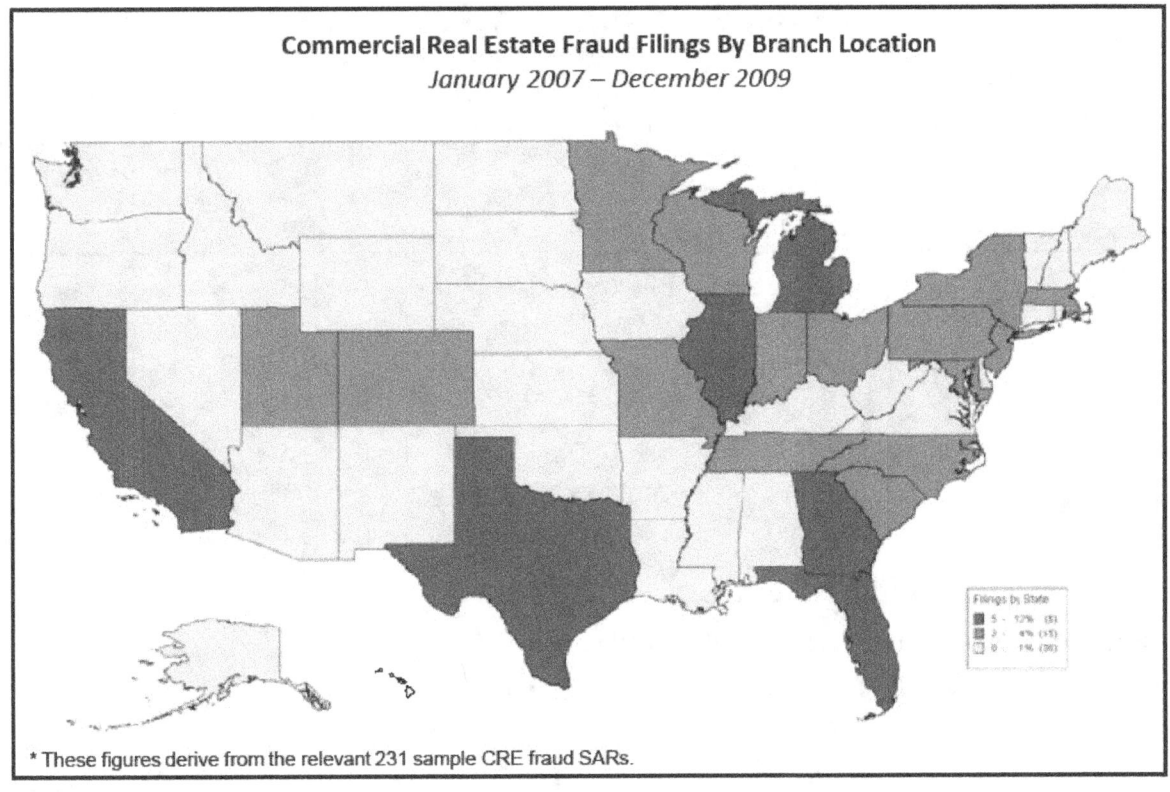

Commercial Real Estate Fraud Filings By Branch Location
January 2007 – December 2009

* These figures derive from the relevant 231 sample CRE fraud SARs.

Fraud Locations by Population[53]

Using Census Bureau population and BSA data, the following maps show the number of SAR filings by state per one million people based on filer branch and subject address.[54] As Graph A4 shows, most states had one or fewer branch filings per one million inhabitants. However, Georgia, Wyoming, Alaska, Maine, North Dakota, and Michigan each had around two branch filings per one million people.

GRAPH A4

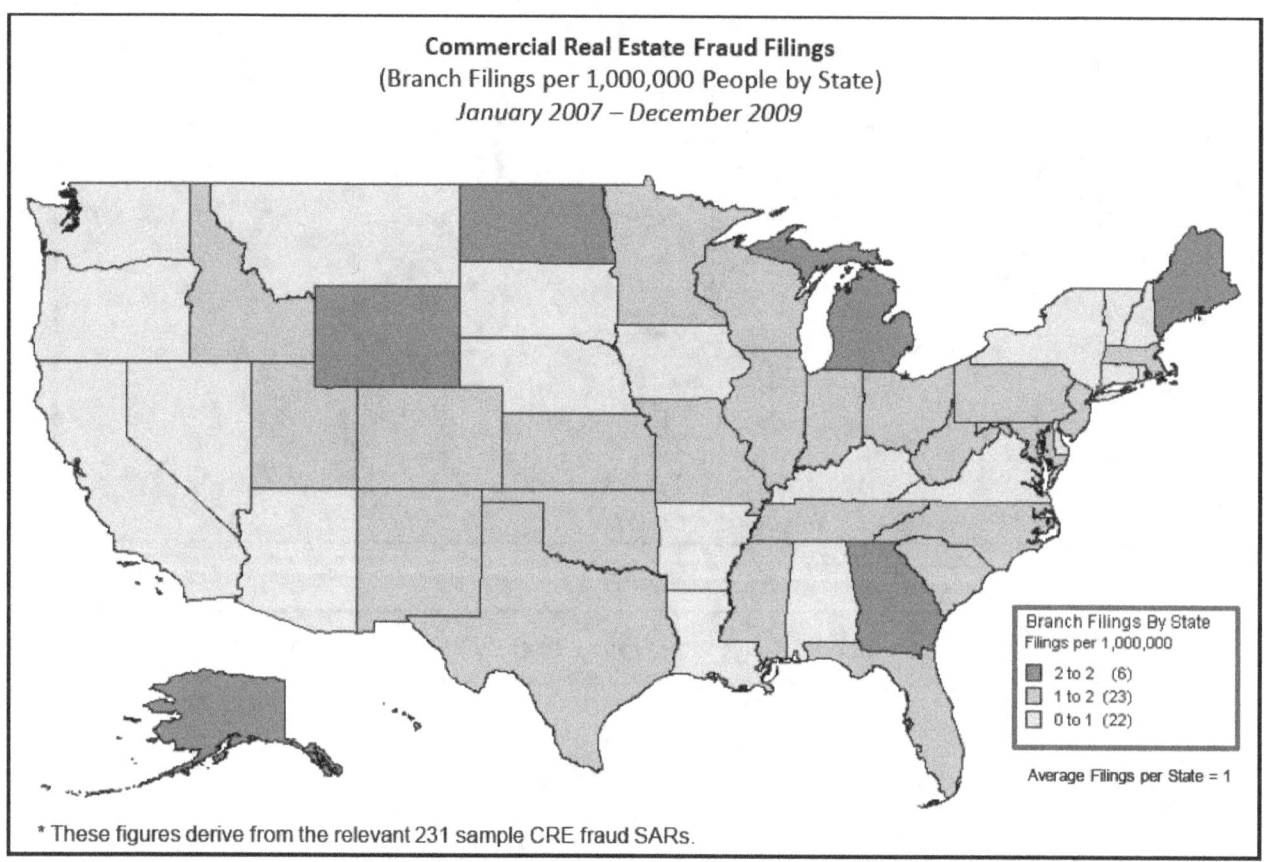

Commercial Real Estate Fraud Filings
(Branch Filings per 1,000,000 People by State)
January 2007 – December 2009

Branch Filings By State
Filings per 1,000,000

2 to 2 (6)
1 to 2 (23)
0 to 1 (22)

Average Filings per State = 1

* These figures derive from the relevant 231 sample CRE fraud SARs.

---

53. Regional population figures are from the 2000 census.

54. Maps also include SAR filings for the District of Columbia.

Filers reported on average two subjects per million state residents. Graph A5 indicates that Georgia had the highest number of reported subjects with 11 subjects per one million people. Locations with the next highest counts included the District of Columbia (seven filings) and Illinois (six filings) followed by Tennessee, Alaska, Michigan, and Florida with nearly five filings each.

GRAPH A5

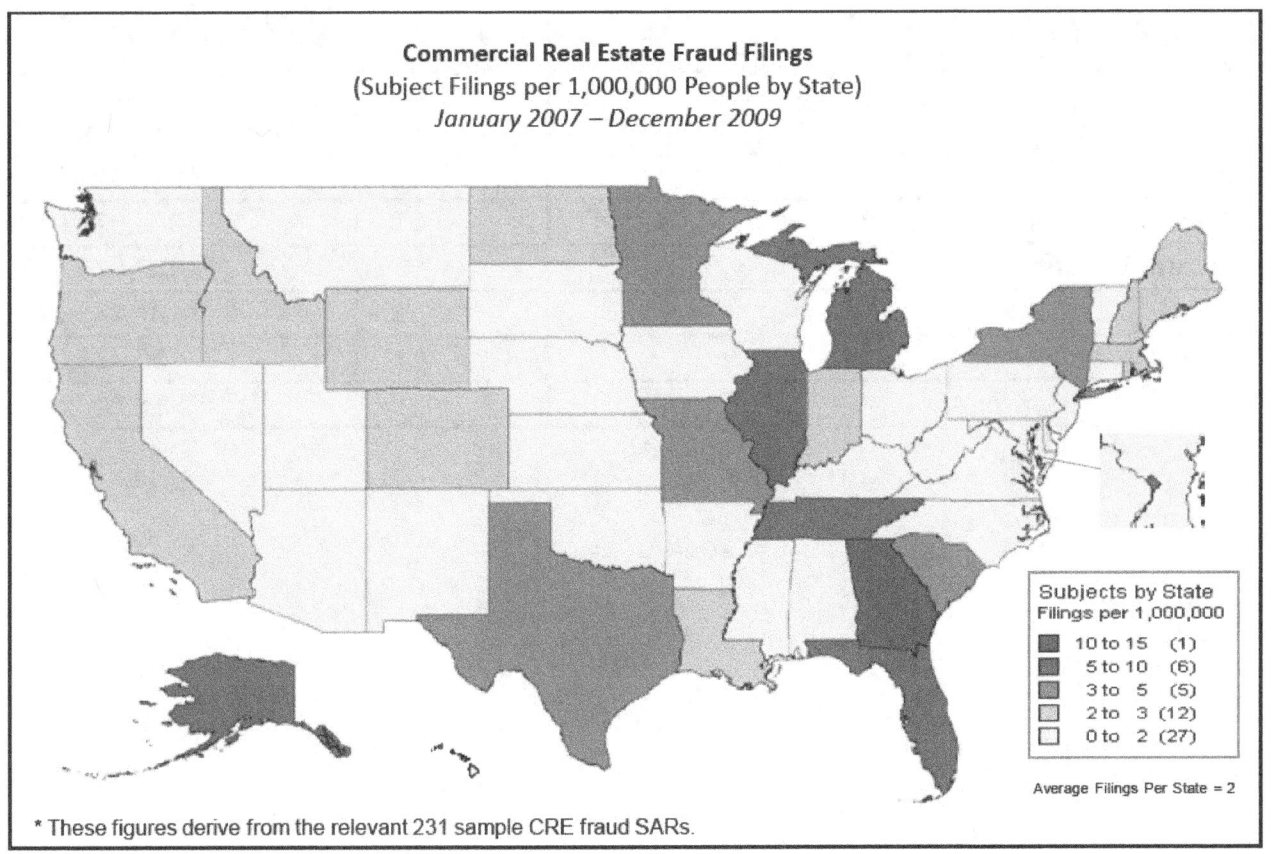

Commercial Real Estate Fraud Filings
(Subject Filings per 1,000,000 People by State)
January 2007 – December 2009

Subjects by State
Filings per 1,000,000

10 to 15	(1)
5 to 10	(6)
3 to 5	(5)
2 to 3	(12)
0 to 2	(27)

Average Filings Per State = 2

* These figures derive from the relevant 231 sample CRE fraud SARs.

Primary Federal Regulators

Filers noted the Federal Deposit Insurance Corporation (FDIC) as their primary federal regulator in 48 percent of all CRE fraud SARs.

TABLE A5

Commercial Real Estate Fraud SARs Filers' Primary Federal Regulators *(January 2007 - December 2009)*		
Regulator	*SARs*[55]	*Suspicious Activity Amount*[56]
FDIC	48%	$26,864,237
Office of the Comptroller of the Currency (OCC)	21%	$1,005,977,010
Federal Reserve	19%	$602,913,487
Office of Thrift Supervision	9%	$107,483,771
National Credit Union Administration	1%	$5,486,051
Unspecified	1%	$3,200,000

---

55. Due to rounding, percentages do not total 100 percent.

56. The highest amounts reported involved advance fee schemes. Two filers regulated by the OCC reported advance fee schemes for $780 million and another filer regulated by the Federal Reserve reported an advance fee scheme for $500 million.

Narrative Review

Analysts reviewed the narratives of the relevant 231 CRE fraud SARs from 2007-2009 to obtain a more comprehensive understanding of CRE-related fraud schemes and to identify additional trends and patterns. The following section provides a snapshot of suspicious activities, financing methods and purposes, and CRE sectors. All figures and statistics in this section derive from the 231 CRE fraud SARs.

Overview of Suspicious Activities

Table A6 lists the kinds of suspicious activities described in CRE fraud SAR narratives.

TABLE A6

Commercial Real Estate Fraud SARs Activities Described in Narratives (January 2007 - December 2009)	
Activity	**SARs[57]**
False Documents	42%
Misappropriation of Funds	29%
Collusion - Bank Insider	19%
False Statements	15%
Theft	10%
Collusion - Non Bank Insider	10%
Other	8%
Non-Disclosure to Lender	9%
Ownership Transfers	7%
Sold Collateral	5%
Flipping	5%
Advance Fee Schemes	3%

---

57. Some filers reported multiple types of suspicious activities within one SAR narrative. Therefore, percentages exceed 100 percent.

Filers most commonly cited misrepresentations involving documentation, false statements, misappropriation of funds, and collusion involving bank insiders as suspicious activities. Filers reported the following suspicious activities.

False Documents:

Filers cited suspected misrepresentations involving documentation in 42 percent of SARs. Common misrepresentations included fraudulent rent rolls, tax documentation, financial statements, identification documents, appraisals, and forged signatures. Filers suspected that bank insiders sometimes colluded by providing false documents to loan approval committees, approving loan disbursements after reviewing fraudulent invoices, and submitting incomplete paperwork. Additional activities included false claims of property ownership.

Misappropriation of Funds:

Filers suspected misappropriation of funds in 29 percent of CRE fraud SARs, indicating diversion of funds for personal profit or support to businesses facing insolvency. Filers discovered the suspicious activity after finding undisclosed liens on collateral, fraudulent disbursement documentation, and/or inspecting sites with little or no construction work performed. Over half the SARs describing misappropriation of funds were for transactions under $1 million.

Commercial Real Estate Financing

Although filers reported on various forms of CRE financing in SAR narratives, 58 percent of the narratives described loans as the CRE financing mechanism.[58] Many filers referenced specific types of loan arrangements, including lines of credit and mortgages. They also described borrower use of CRE as collateral for financing unrelated to the acquisition or development of commercial property.[59] However, filers most frequently stated that loans were for construction and/or acquisition of property.

---

58. Filers reported multiple types of financing within the SAR narratives. Therefore, percentages exceed 100 percent.

59. Examples cited in SARs include the use of CRE as collateral for vehicle and equipment loans.

TABLE A7

Commercial Real Estate Fraud SARs Loan Purpose Described in SAR Narratives (January 2007 - December 2009)	
Purpose	**SARs**
Construction	34%
Acquisition	25%
Mortgage	8%
Land Development	7%
Renovation	6%
Working Capital	6%
Refinance	5%
Unspecified	9%

Commercial Real Estate Sectors

Filers indicated the CRE sector involved in the suspicious activity in only 56 percent of CRE fraud narratives. These sectors were most frequently retail and multi-family properties.[60]

TABLE A8

Commercial Real Estate Fraud SARs Property Sector in SAR Narratives (January 2007 - December 2009)	
Sector	**SARs**
Retail	15%
Multi-family	15%
Single-family	11%
Office	5%
Hospitality[61]	5%
Industrial	3%
Healthcare	3%

---

60. Some filers reported on properties from multiple sectors, whereas other filers referred to "commercial real estate" or "commercial property," but not to a specific sector.

61. Hospitality includes businesses engaged in both the lodging and food service industry.

Retail:

Filers described retail properties in 15 percent of SAR narratives. Retail properties included stores, gas stations, car lots, and shopping centers. Frequently reported activities included suspected misrepresentations involving documentation and false statements.

Multi-family:

Filers described multi-family properties, including apartments and condominiums, in 15 percent of CRE fraud SARs. Frequently reported activities included misrepresentations involving documentation, bank insider collusion, and misappropriation of funds.

Other Narrative Details

Regulatory or Law Enforcement References:

Filers referenced contact with regulators or law enforcement in 22 percent of CRE fraud SAR narratives. In some instances, law enforcement or regulators contacted a depository institution, which in turn launched an internal investigation. In other instances, filers contacted law enforcement or regulators about suspicious activities. Filers referenced a multitude of federal regulatory agencies, federal law enforcement agencies, local police departments, and state banking authorities.

Misrepresentations Causing Loan Application Denials:

Filers referenced denied loan applications in 7 percent of the SAR narratives, most commonly for misrepresentation of rent rolls to make it appear that rental income was higher than it actually was. Most denied applications involved borrowers attempting to refinance properties. Filers discovered many of these activities through site inspections and verification of rental income from tax records. Other suspicious activities included:

- tax misrepresentations

- suspicious business proposals/advance fee schemes

- fraudulent social security numbers

- nonresponsive requests for additional information

- questionable property ownership

Participation Loans:

Filers referenced participation loans in 4 percent of the SAR narratives. The values of these participation loans ranged from approximately $4 million to $110 million, and the loan purposes included acquisition, land development, and construction.[62] In connection with these loans, filers suspected misrepresentations involving documentation, ownership, and liabilities, as well as undisclosed use of side agreements, overinflated appraisals, and real estate brokers who sold a nonexistent participation loan.[63]

Flipping:

Filers referenced flipping properties in 4 percent of the SAR narratives. Several filers reported flips taking place within the same day, or within a close timeframe, between family members or related business entities. Two filers reported that land developers with pre-sale contracts for condominium sales devised side agreements with other condominium buyers to sell properties in order to qualify for loan disbursements. Buyers then flipped the property back to the borrower for a predetermined price or to another buyer before closing. Other filers reported bank insiders for violations of bank policy and issuing numerous delinquent loans.

---

62. These figures derive from the value of the whole loans, not individual participation amounts. In cases where filers reported only their individual participation amounts in the suspicious activity amount field of the SARs, analysts determined the whole loan amounts from information provided in the SAR narratives.

63. Filers described side agreements as private deals conducted between sellers and borrowers outside of known loan arrangements. The side agreements negatively affected the value of the CRE collateral.

www.FinCEN.gov